My most grateful thanks go to the families who generously gave their time and energy to this book. It would not have been possible without their help. Special thanks to the individuals and institutions who assisted in making the book possible: Dr. Oscar Cohen, Adrianne Robins, and the Lexington School for the Deaf; Jo Dillenbeck and the New York City Department of Education; The Rusk Institute of Rehabilitation Medicine; Kathryn Simic and the Cooke Center for Learning and Development; Linda Frankenmolle; Susan Scheer; Stephanie Nolan; Susan Romano-Silva; Patricia McCaul; and Lisa Slomovicz.–L.D.

Published in the United States of America by Star Bright Books, Inc., New York. The name Star Bright Books and the Star Bright Books logo are registered trademarks of Star Bright Books, Inc. Please visit www.starbrightbooks.com.

Designed by Design Press.

ISBN 1-887734-80-5

Printed in China 9 8 7 6 5 4 3 2 1

Page 27, top photo: Screen grab from the Nickelodeon program entitled "Kablam!" © 2005 Viacom International, Inc. All rights reserved. Nickelodeon, Kablam! and all related titles, logos and characters are trademarks of Viacom International Inc.

Library of Congress Cataloging-in-Publication Data

Dwight, Laura.
  Brothers and sisters / by Laura Dwight.
     p. cm.
  ISBN 1-887734-80-5
  1. Children with disabilities--Juvenile literature. 2. Children with disabilities--Family relationships--Juvenile literature. 3. Brothers and sisters. I. Title.

RJ137.D95 2005
362.4'083--dc22

2005006517

Brothers

and

Sisters

By
Laura
Dwight

Star Bright Books
New York

I am Shannon, and I am five years old. These are my brothers Hunter and Kellen. Hunter is four, and Kellen is two years old. When Kellen was growing in our mother's tummy, part of one of his arms didn't grow. Kellen calls that arm "Pinky" and he can do many things with it. Some children think that Pinky hurts Kellen, but it doesn't. His arm feels fine to him, just the way yours does.

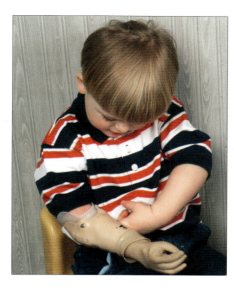

Kellen has a special hand and arm called a prosthesis. Kellen can make the hand open and close by moving the muscles on Pinky.

Here are some of the things Kellen can do when he plays with us. Kellen uses Pinky to steady the bowl when he drops the ball in.

Kellen can use his prosthesis to pick up little things, so he can play a game that has small pieces. Because Kellen is growing, he has a new prosthesis. He is just getting used to it.

Kellen loves to bounce
high. He holds Pinky
up to help him balance.

We have a lot of fun together. We like to
roughhouse with our dad and pile on top of him.

Then we show him how we can do somersaults.

When we race,
Kellen takes the lead!

I am Zaire and this is my twin brother, Romare. We are five years old. Romare wears hearing aids to help him hear. I wear leg braces called orthotics to help me walk.

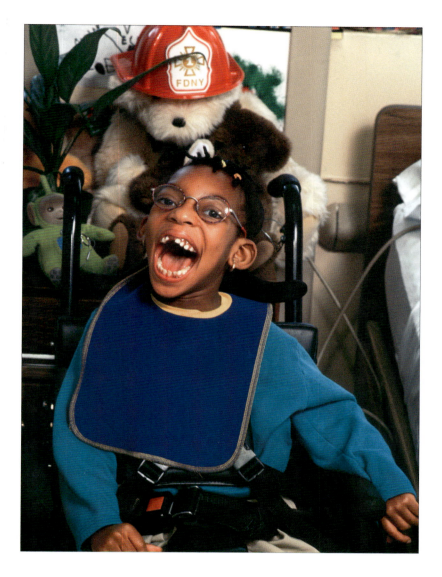

This is our sister, Eubie. She is six. Eubie's brain was hurt when she was born. It is hard for her brain to tell her body what she wants to do. Eubie uses a wheelchair, and she needs help communicating. Eubie can only say a few words. She moves her eyes to show what she wants, uses a computer to say what she wants, and smiles her beautiful smile!

This year Eubie had an operation to make it easier for her to move her legs. Afterwards, she had to stay at the hospital for a long time.

We missed Eubie a lot. Our mom visited her every day. She read books to her, and brought her food from home.

At the hospital, a physical therapist helped Eubie learn how to use her body.

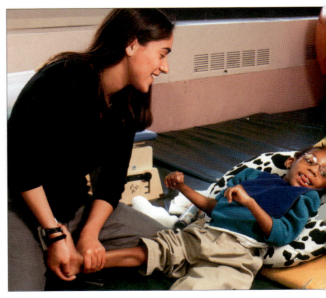

A teacher helped Eubie with her school work.

A speech therapist worked on a communication board with Eubie that helps her say what she wants. This board fits on the front of her wheelchair and can go anywhere with her.

Eubie also learned to use a computer program to say what she wanted. Eubie pressed "Zaire" and "Romare" on the computer. She loved to see our names on the screen!

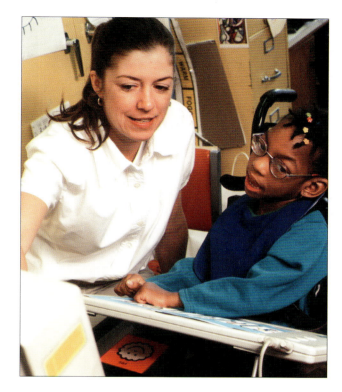

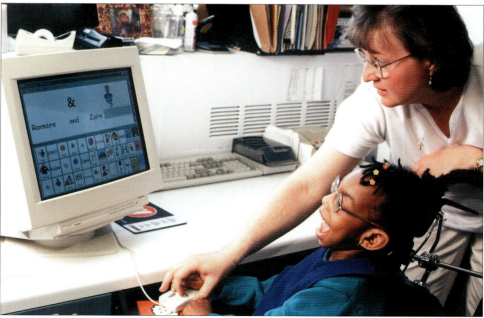

At home, Romare and I made block towers and read books. It wasn't the same without Eubie.

Finally, Eubie came home.

We danced, played games, and read books together. We were so happy to see her!

I am Chloe and this is my brother James. James is twelve, and I am nine. He has always been blind. James says a good thing about being blind is that the world is full of surprises. We spend a lot of time together.

Here we are playing
Chinese checkers, a game
that is usually played
with marbles. This is a
special set. Each color
has a shape so James can
tell where his pieces are.
James makes a map of
the board in his head,
and he wins!

James and I are reading the same book. I am reading a regular printed book, and James is reading a Braille version with his fingertips. Each letter is written in a dot pattern. James can read very quickly, faster than I can read aloud.

James loves to use the computer. There is a device on it that says out loud what is happening on the screen.

Sometimes we just relax and listen to stories on tape.

When we walk outside, James uses a cane with a rolling ball on the tip. Sometimes James walks with his hand on my arm, instead of using the cane. I have to remember to warn him if something he might trip over is coming up.

I am Edwin, and I am the oldest brother in my family. I am thirteen. Willie is next. He is nine, and he has Down syndrome. It takes him a little longer to learn things. Something else is a little different for Willie. Like Kellen, part of him didn't grow when he was in our mother's tummy. His fingers on one hand are shorter than usual, but this doesn't stop him from doing lots of things. My youngest brother is James. He is five, and he and Willie often play and do things together.

Sometimes when I am busy reading or doing homework, Willie and James want me to pay attention to them instead. They can be really annoying, but if they didn't like me, they wouldn't want to play with me.

I collect cards and it takes a lot of time to go through them and organize them.

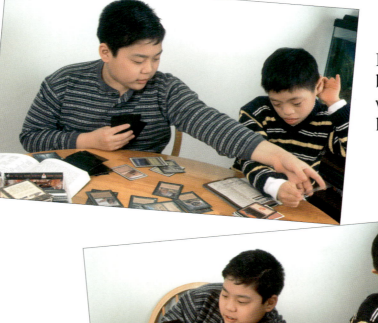

I have to concentrate, but sometimes Willie wants me to play with him instead.

So he grabs my cards, and tries to take them away.

Willie likes it when I play with him. We set up the marble run together.

James and Willie like to ride bikes at the playground.

James and Willie both want to ride the big jeep. Sometimes James has a long turn and doesn't want to give it up. Our father tells James to share and then Willie has a turn.

Our mother teaches Willie and James how to make dumplings.

They work hard, and when they are done, we all have a yummy treat.

I am Jabir, and this is my sister, Najia. She is 10 years old, and I am 8. We both wear hearing aids because we can't hear very well, but Najia cannot hear very much even with them on. She goes to a special school where deaf and hearing-impaired children learn together. I go to a school in the neighborhood. A sign language interpreter helps me understand the teacher. When people sign, they use their hands to communicate instead of their voices. Najia and I speak to each other in sign language. In our home, four languages are used: American sign language, English, Spanish, and Arabic!

We are watching television. On the screen you can see the words that tell us what words and sounds are going on. This is called "closed captioning." A machine connected to the television makes it work.

We sign when we play cards.

Najia loves to use the TTY to talk to her friends. This is a telephone with a keyboard. The conversation happens in words that move across the screen.

The TTY is the only way that Najia can talk to her friends. Sometimes when I try to take a turn, Najia won't let me use it. Our mom comes in and helps us work it out.

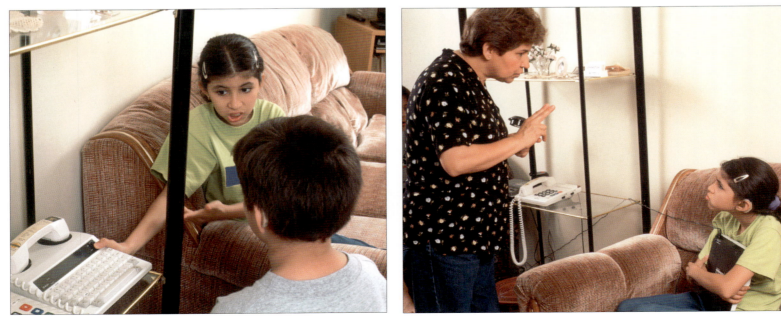

There are lots of things
we like to do together.

Timberrrrr!

I am Sophie, and this is my big brother Charlie. He is seven, and I am four. Charlie loves animals and dinosaurs, and knows a lot about them. He has an amazing memory and can tell you exactly who said what in his favorite movies.

Charlie sometimes needs help from me. When he plays with his animals, he concentrates so hard he forgets about everything around him.

But I know how to get him to do other things.

When Charlie plays games by himself, it is very hard to interrupt him.

I have to work very hard to get his attention, but I always do!

We like to play pretend. I make sure I get a bite!

Outside at the park,
I sneak up to tickle
Charlie's feet.

We have lots
of fun together!

Glossary

<u>Congenital Amputation</u> (Kellen & Willie) Sometimes a person is born with a partial or missing limb. Kellen was born without part of one of his arms and Willie was born with fingers that are shorter than usual. Both of them have found ways to do the things they need to do. For example, Willie learned to write with his right hand even though it was difficult for him to do so. Some people, like Kellen, have an artificial arm, leg, or hand (a prosthesis) to help them.

<u>Asperger's Syndrome</u> (Charlie) Asperger's syndrome is a disorder similar to autism. People with this disorder perceive things differently. They have normal to high intelligence, but may have difficulty making friends and they find it hard to tell if people are being sarcastic or funny. They may become experts in areas that interest them. They might also be very sensitive to loud noises or bright lights, or might not like how some things feel, like sand in a sandbox or scratchy clothes.

<u>Blindness</u> (James) Some people are blind, which means they have no vision at all. Blind people use their senses of touch and hearing to do many things, and some use a cane or a guide dog to help them.

<u>Down Syndrome</u> (Willie) People with Down syndrome are born with an extra chromosome. Chromosomes are the little bits of information that tell our bodies how they should be formed. People with Down syndrome are like other people. There are some things they can do well and others they have difficulty with. Some can learn to do many things, but need a little longer to do so.

<u>Deafness and Hearing Impairment</u> (Najia, Jabir, and Romare) People who are deaf cannot hear. People who are hearing-impaired have some hearing and can be helped to hear more with a hearing aid or cochlear implant. Some deaf and hearing-impaired people use sign language to communicate. Some use trained dogs to assist them and use special devices like TTY telephones and closed-captioned television so they can read what is being said.

<u>Cerebral Palsy</u> (Eubie and Zaire) Cerebral palsy may be caused by a brain injury during birth. People with cerebral palsy may have physical or mental disabilities. Some are very affected by it, like Eubie, and some, like Zaire, are not as affected. Each part of the brain has a different job and the part that gets hurt causes different problems. People with cerebral palsy may need to use braces or walkers to help them walk, while others use wheelchairs or scooters to get around.

Resources

UNITED STATES

Visual Impairments

American Foundation for the Blind
11 Penn Plaza, Suite 300
New York, NY 10001
800-232-5463
http://www.afb.org

Lighthouse International
111 E 59th Street
New York, NY 10022-1202
800-829-0500
http://www.lighthouse.org

Congenital Amputation

LimbDifferences.org
http://www.limbdifferences.org

I-CAN
International Child Amputee Network
701 Briarwood
Abilene, TX 79603
http://www.child-amputee.net

Asperger's Syndrome and Autism

OASIS On-line Asperger's Syndrome
Information and Support
http://www.udel.edu/bkirby/asperger

Autism Society of America
7910 Woodmont Avenue, Suite 300
Bethesda, MD 20814-3067
800-328-8476
http://www.autism-society.org

Hearing Impairments

American Society for Deaf Children
P.O. Box 3355
Gettysburg, PA 17325
800-942-2732 (v/tty)
http://www.deafchildren.org

American Speech, Language,
Hearing Association
10801 Rockville Pike
Rockville, MD 20852
800-638-8255
http://www.asha.org

Down Syndrome

National Down Syndrome Congress
1370 Center Drive, Suite 102
Atlanta, GA 30338
800-232-6372
http://www.ndsccenter.org

National Down Syndrome Society
666 Broadway, 8th Floor
New York, NY 10012-2317
800-221-4602
http://www.ndss.org

Cerebral Palsy

UCP (United Cerebral
Palsy Associations)
1660 L Street NW, Suite 700
Washington, DC 20036-5602
800-872-5827
http://www.ucp.org

General Disabilities

National Dissemination Center for
Children with Disabilities
P.O. Box 1492
Washington, DC 20013
800-695-0285 (v/tty)
http://www.nichcy.org

UNITED KINGDOM

Visual Impairment

Royal National Institute of the Blind
105 Judd Street
London WC1H 9NE
Tel: 0207 388 1266
http://www.rnib.org.uk

Congenital Amputation

REACH
P.O. Box 54
Helston, Cornwall, TR13 8WD
Tel: 0845 130 6225
http://www.reach.org.uk

Asperger's Syndrome and Autism

The Autistic Society
393 City Road
London EC1V ING
Tel: 0207 833 2299
http://www.nas.org.uk

Hearing Impairments

Royal National Institute for Deaf People
19-23 Featherstone Street
London EC1Y 8SL
Tel: 0207 296 8000
http://www.rnid.org.uk

National Deaf Children's Society
15 Dufferin Street
London EC1Y 8UR
Tel: 0808 800 8880
http://www.ndcs.org.uk

Down Syndrome

Down's Syndrome Association
Langdon Down Centre
2a Langdon Park
Teddington TW11 9PS
Tel: 0845 230 0372
http://www.downs-syndrome.org.uk

Cerebral Palsy

Scope/Cerebral Palsy Helpline
P.O. Box 833
Milton Keynes MK12 5NY
Tel: 0808 800 3333
http://www.scope.org.uk

General Disabilities

The Council for Disabled Children
8 Wakley Street
London EC1V 7QE
Tel: 0207 843 1900
http://www.ncb.org.uk/cdc

CANADA

Visual Impairment

The Canadian National
Institute for the Blind
1929 Bayview Avenue
Toronto, ON M4G 3E8
416-486-2500
http://www.cnib.ca

Congenital Amputation

Champ Program for Children
The War Amps
2827 Riverside Drive
Ottawa, ON K1V OC4
800-267-4023
http://www.waramps.ca/champ

Asperger's Syndrome and Autism

Autism Treatment Services of Canada
404-94th Street SE
Calgary, AB T2J OE8
403-253-6961
http://www.autism.ca

Hearing Impairments

The Canadian Hearing Society
271 Spadina Road
Toronto, ON M5R 2V3
416-928-2500 (v) 416-964-0023 (tty)
http://www.chs.ca

Down Syndrome

Canadian Down Syndrome Society
811-14th Street NW
Calgary, AB T2N 2A4
800-883-5608
http://www.cdss.ca

Cerebral Palsy

The Cerebral Palsy Assc. of Canada
10-8180 Macleod Trail S
Calgary, AB T2H 2B8
800-363-2807
http://www.fcip.ca/CP

General Disabilities

Disability weblinks
http://www.disabilityweblinks.ca

Abilityonline.org
1120 Finch Avenue W, Suite 104
Toronto ON M3J 3H7
866-650-6207
http://www.ablelink.org